Tyrannosaurus Tex

Tyrannosaurus Tex

❖❖❖

by Dr. Bob, D.D.
(Doctor of Dinosaurs)

illustrations by Nurse Mary

❖❖❖

State House Press
1989

Copyright 1989 State House Press

Library of Congress Cataloging-in-Publication Data

Bob, Dr., 1941-
    Tyrannosaurus Tex / by Dr. Bob ; illustrations by Nurse
Mary.
        p.   cm.
    Summary: Relates the adventures of a young dinosaur
growing up in Texas. Includes a glossary of dinosaurs
describing their physical characteristics and natural habitat.
        ISBN 0-938349-38-4
        [1. Dinosaurs—Fiction]   I. Mary, Nurse, 1943-   ill.
II. Title.
PZ7.B632Ty 1989
[E]—dc19   89-4225
                                                           CIP
                                                            AC

*Back Cover: Photograph of Dr. Bob and Nurse Mary at work in their "clinic"
    for sick and wounded dinosaurs.*

        Photo by Harry Roberts; toy manufactured by Illuminations.

Printed in the United States of America

State House Press
P.O. Box 15247
Austin, Texas 78761

For Sarah

and the Other Children of the World

Long, long ago in a land not far away, a young couple roamed about looking for a place to settle. They were about to have their first child.

"We need a place with a lot of room," said Mr. Rex. "Rhode Island and even Maine are much too small for us. Let's go to Texas!"

Mrs. Rex was very happy to move because they needed more space with a baby on the way. "That's a wonderful idea, dear," she said to her husband.

So off they went to their new home.

When they arrived in Texas, the baby was almost due. They rushed to the hospital, Prehistoric General. After a short time, Mrs. Rex delivered her egg, just over a foot long. Then, after a long wait and much care, the new baby arrived.

"How cute he is," said the nurses.

"How tiny he is," said Mrs. Rex.

"I want to hold him too," said Mr. Rex. They sent birth announcements to their friends.

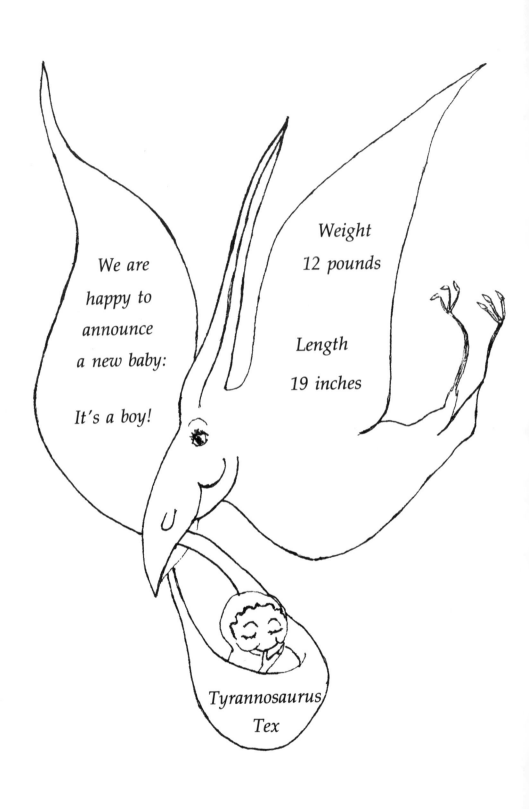

Tex was a healthy and happy baby. He smiled at everyone. Tex waved his arms and kicked his legs. His proud parents spent hours looking into the nursery, watching the nurses care for him. Mrs. Rex eagerly waited for the wonderful times when the nurses brought Tex to her room. There she learned to take care of him. He loved to eat and make faces and gurgle. Mommy and Daddy had such a happy time burping their baby.

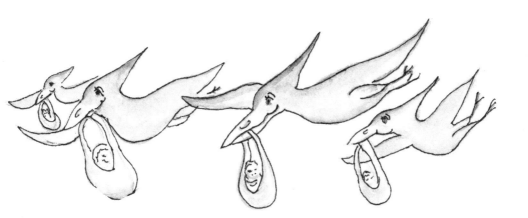

In the same nursery, a baby named
Broncilla had been born on the same day as Tex.
She was a large dinosaur baby with a small,
pretty face. She saw that Tex looked different

from her. Broncilla did not want to play with him. This hurt Tex's feelings, but he kept trying to play with Broncilla.

After several days in the hospital, the nurses prepared Tex to go home. They bundled him warmly for the short trip. Mr. and Mrs. Rex gently placed Tex in a crib near their bed.

They were afraid to leave him. What if he got hungry, or cold, or wet? Would he keep breathing? They had never realized what changes a baby would bring! Now he became the center of attention.

For several weeks he slept in his parents' room, even though they had prepared a nursery with special wallpaper for him. Finally, they put him in his own room.

PREHISTORIC GENERAL

Of course, they left the doors open. Every
night Mrs. Rex rocked Tex to sleep in his
cradle, softly singing a dinosaur lullaby song.

"Rock-a-by Te-ex,
You are so sweet;
When dinosaurs sleep,
In dreamland they meet;
Where they all play,
And have lots of fun;
Where wishes come true,
And love makes them one."

It seemed everyone wanted to see the new baby. He looked so cute and cuddly! Grandma Rex came all the way from Montana to see him, and to help Mr. and Mrs. Rex take care of him. Mrs. Rex still felt tired from the delivery and welcomed Grandma Rex's visit. They gave Tex warm baths, fed him, and changed his diapers.

Grandpa Rex couldn't come right away. So they sent him pictures. He sent Tex his first toy, a small furry Maiasaura. Tex loved his new toy and even slept with it. Friends and neighbors brought gifts too.

Broncilla's mother often babysat with Tex. She brought Broncilla along with her. At times, the two babies looked at each other and cooed.

Tex liked to explore. He got into everything after he learned to crawl. He surprised his parents by climbing out of his crib twice. They could not keep up with him. They made sure he wouldn't go near anything that would hurt him.

His parents watched him very closely.
Once he got into Mrs. Rex's pancake batter.
What a mess! They couldn't be mad at him
for too long. He always made them laugh.

Mr. Rex hurried home from work
to play with Tex. How happy they
were together! Mr. Rex played
piggyback with his new son.
Mrs. Rex watched and they
all had fun.

On Tex's first birthday, he tired of
crawling and wanted to walk. He pulled
himself up and tried to take a step. He fell
down, and had a hard time pulling himself
up again.

Mrs. Rex called to Mr. Rex, "Dear, Tex is
trying to walk!" Mr. Rex ran into the room
and, when he saw what happened, he smiled.

Then he helped Tex up and held him by his
short arms. Tex tried to walk again and
this time he took his first step.

Mr. and Mrs. Rex became so excited that they almost forgot to catch Tex when he fell again. They caught him and made sure that he did not get hurt. Soon, he walked all by himself. His parents took more pictures for Grandma and Grandpa Rex.

Tex grew quickly in the love of his home. He stood 6 feet tall by the time he reached age three. Tex was about the size of a small truck. He liked to play with tyranno twigs and small stuffed animals.

Tex had a hard time making friends because the other children in the neighborhood thought he looked different. He was too tall they said, and his nose grew so long. What a funny looking kid, they said. Only Broncilla wanted to be his friend. He had first met her in the nursery. They had played together when they were babies.

"I'm so sorry for not liking you before," she said. "I had never met a Tyrannosaurus before and you scared me. Now that I've gotten to know what a nice dinosaur you are, it doesn't matter. Let's be friends."

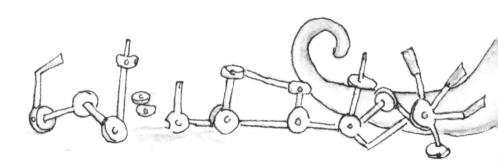

When Tex became four years old his parents gave him a big birthday party. Some of the children in the neighborhood no longer feared Tex and were invited to the party. They all brought gifts. Mrs. Rex led the children in a game of pin the tail on the Ultrasaurus.

Then Mrs. Rex brought in the cake
with the four candles on it. Tex made a
wish and blew out the candles.

Tex's friends all wanted to know what he
wished, but he wouldn't tell. Later, he told
Broncilla that he wished that even more
children would like him.

He opened his gifts and was very pleased with the space toys. He was interested in rockets and astronauts.

Best of all, his parents had bought him a beautiful new red tricycle. Tex thanked everyone for coming and for the great presents they had given him.

"Happy birthday to you,
Happy birthday to you,
Happy birthday dear Te-ex,
Happy birthday to you."

Tex couldn't wait to try out his new tricycle. After many tries, he got on and tried to pedal. He slipped, fell off, and had the hardest time trying to get up again. Finally, he got back on the trike and pedaled. Now he couldn't steer it in the right direction and slammed into the bushes.

He called for help and Mr. Rex came running. He pulled the trike with Tex on it out of the bushes. He told Tex he would be all right. He just needed some practice.

After several days of practice, Tex could start, stop, and steer his tricycle. His parents were so proud of Tex that they bought him a new bell and handlebar ribbons for his trike.

Soon after his fourth birthday, Tex's
parents thought he was ready for preschool.
They wanted him at home, but also
felt that, as an only child, he needed to
spend more time with other children. They
seemed a bit sad to bring him to school,
but they felt proud of him and happy too.

Tex knew his parents would come back to get him.

He was glad when he saw his new classmates. He liked his teacher, Ms. Steggy, right away. What a pretty bright, blue bonnet she wore. Broncilla was happy to see him, but the other children did not like Tex.

They stayed away from him. They said
that their parents had told them that
all Tyrannosauruses were mean.

Tex kept trying to make friends with
the other children. He was very smart and
lots of fun. Ms. Steggy tried hard to get the
other children to like Tex. She gave him a
lot of attention. When one of his classmates
made fun of him, Broncilla put her arm
around Tex.

One day Ms. Steggy gave a special
lesson. "Now children, you all know that a
well-mannered dinosaur never drags his
tail. Look at how nicely Tex holds his
tail—high up. He is a good example
for all of us." She patted Tex with
her large tail and he felt wonderful.
The class now liked Tex.

Tricy, the little boy Triceratops said,
"You seem different from the other Tyrannosauruses. You are so much fun and well-
mannered. Maybe you could be our
friend."

When Tex's mother came for him after
school, she could tell that something great
had happened. He told her that the other
children finally liked him. This made her
very happy and she gave him a big dinosaur
hug.

Later that week Tex felt sick. His head
hurt, he coughed, and he felt too weak to
get out of bed. His thick skin broke out in
scaly, itchy bumps.

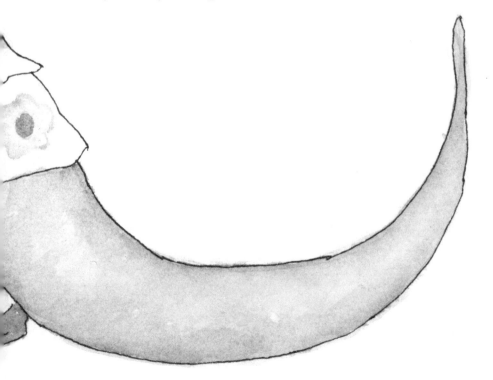

His parents became worried and called Dr. Trachowitz, the family doctor. After looking at Tex, the doctor said that he had chicken pox. The doctor gave Tex medicine to help the itching, and told him to drink lots of fern juice.

Tex got well fast with the good care of Dr. Trachowitz and his parents. He missed being with his friends. Broncilla often brought games and toys. His father bought him a new rocket and some puzzles. He enjoyed playing with them. Soon, the itching disappeared, and Tex wanted to go to school.

When Tex went back to school, all the children said, "Hi!" They told him that they missed him. How good it felt to have so many friends!

On this beautiful day, Ms. Steggy took the children to the park where there was a very nice playground. Tex and his new friend, Tricy, went on the see-saw. Tex went all the way down and Tricy went all

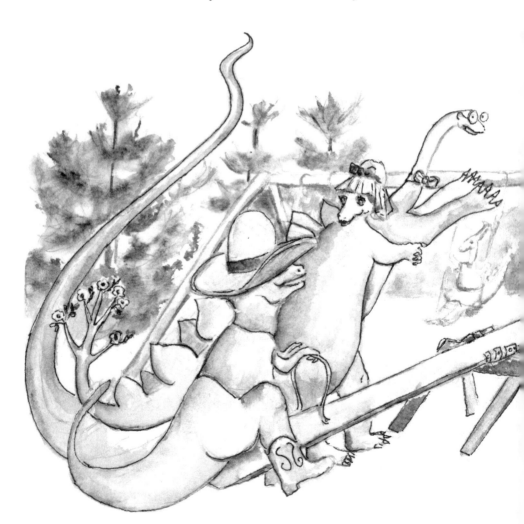

the way up—and stayed there. Tricy got scared, stuck up so high. "Tex, let me down, please!"

Tex wanted to help but didn't know what to do. He knew that if he got off, Tricy would come down with a crash and get hurt. He called Ms. Steggy who came right away.

"I think I know what the problem is fellas," she said. "Tex weighs a bit more than Tricy, about 1,000 pounds. Tricy, please move all the way to the back edge of the see-saw and Tex move in a bit."

They did what their teacher said. Sure enough, Tricy came slowly down, touched the ground, and then went up again. What

fun! Broncilla thought they looked silly.
She liked the swing. Their friend Dipply,
the little diplodocus, loved the slide.

The rest of the children had a great
time playing ball and hide-and-seek. For a
special treat, Ms. Steggy took the children
to the Fossil County Amusement Park for a
ride on the Saurosel.

That evening, Mrs. Rex made their favorite dinner, spaghetti, while Mr. Rex read the paper, *The Fossil County Times.* Mr. Rex liked to cook, too. Sometimes he and Tex prepared the meal. Tex wanted to help his parents, so he did his chores around the house. They were so good to him.

As he ate his dinner, his front tooth became loose and hurt a little. His Mom and Dad told him that he would lose the tooth, but grow a new one. After he chewed some more spaghetti, the tooth came out.

They put it under his pillow for the dinosaur tooth fairy. The next morning, he found a shiny, new quarter under his pillow. The tooth had vanished.

Tex was now six years old, and finishing kindergarten. After school one day, Tex invited his friends Tricy and Dipply to his house to play. Tricy was very playful and liked to tease Tex. Dipply was very nice and quieter than Tricy. They had a lot of fun together. Tex shared his toys with them, even his space toys and trike.

After they left, Tex was alone in the yard riding on his trike. Suddenly, something ran across his path. It looked so little, and moved so fast. Tex's mother had told him never to leave the yard. She could watch him there. He was so curious about the little Othnielia that he forgot what his mother said. Tex followed him on his trike.

Tex pedaled his trike as fast as he could after the Othnielia. He could see this fellow had a small head, a beak, large eyes, and hands with five fingers. He seemed a little over two feet long, and Tex now rose to eight feet tall, stretched twenty feet long, and weighed 6,000 pounds. He was about the size of a school classroom.

How cute and interesting, thought Tex as he hurried after the Othnielia. As Tex got farther and farther into the forest, he began to have a bad feeling. He had no idea where he was.

Suddenly, the Othnielia stopped, turned toward Tex, and said in a little voice, "Do you know what you are?"

"Yes," said Tex. "I am a little boy Tyrannosaurus."

"Wrong," said the Othnielia. "You are a *lost* little boy Tyrannosaurus." And he ran away.

The sun disappeared and the sky darkened. Tex got scared, and tired, and hungry. He missed his parents and his home so much. He sat on a big rock, and began to cry.

Tex's parents became very upset when they could not find him. Broncilla helped them look.

"Tex Rex, where are you?" she cried. "Oh, my very best friend! What could have happened to you?"

They looked all over, but he was nowhere to be found. The Rexes called the police and Inspector Anky came right away.

"Do not worry Sir . . .Ma'am. We have ways of finding lost Tyrannosauruses. Since they are so tall, they are best seen from the air. I've had cases like this before."

He polished his magnifying glass to
look for clues. He sent out Captain
Pteranodon of the Texas Rangers to lead
the way. Then he gathered together all of
Tex's friends, and began THE GREAT
DINOSAUR BALLOON SEARCH.

That night Tex could not sleep.
Strange sounds filled the night.
He knew that dinosaurs lived
there who could
hurt him.

He wondered what his parents and friends were doing. Were they looking for him? Would they give up if they could not find him?

In the morning, the sun lit up the beautiful forest. Tex saw something move far away in the sky. As it came closer, he could see that it was a balloon. Inside the basket, hanging below the balloon, he saw a familiar shape—

Broncilla!

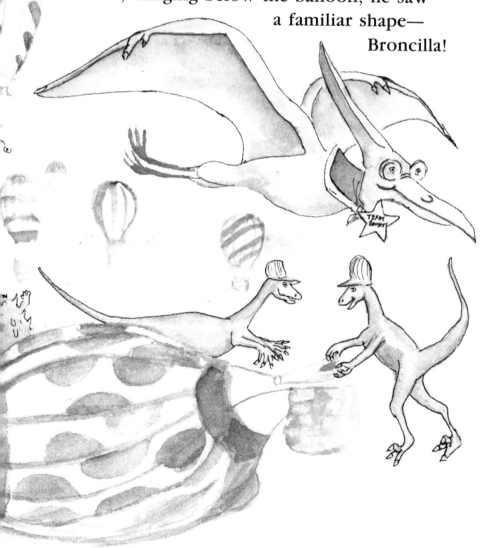

"Broncilla, Broncilla!" he shouted.
"Here I am."

"Thank goodness you are all right,"
she said. "We have been looking all over
for you. Now climb in the basket with me,
and let's go home."

After a short trip, they landed in his
backyard. All his friends clapped and looked
very happy to see him again. His Mommy

and Daddy hugged Tex for a long time,
and told him how worried they had been.

"I'm so sorry," Tex cried. "I'll never
wander off again. I promise to stay real close."

"It's okay, honey," said Mrs. Rex.
"You have learned a lesson and we are just
glad to have you back."

They all had a big WELCOME HOME
TEX party.

List of Characters

Tyrannosaurus Tex - also known as T. Tex or Tex Rex (Male)
Mr. Rex - Tyrannosaurus
Mrs. Rex - Tyrannosaurus
Broncilla - Brontosaurus (Female)
Grandma Rex - Tyrannosaurus
Grandpa Rex - Tyrannosaurus
Ms. Steggy - Stegosaurus
Tricy - Triceratops (Male)
Dr. Trachowitz - Trachodon or Anatosaurus (Male duckbill but not a quack)
Dipply - Diplodocus (Male)
Inspector Anky - Ankylosaurus (Male)
Captain Pteranodon of the Texas Rangers - Pteranodon (Male)
The Othnielia - Othnielia

Dinosaur Glossary

Ankylosaurus (an-KL-low-sawr-us). This dinosaur had spines and bone plates. It looked like a tank and ate plants. The tail was long and looked like a club. It was 25 feet long, 6 feet wide and 4 feet tall. It weighed about ten thousand pounds. Ankylosaurus lived in the U.S.A. (Montana) and Canada.

Brontosaurus (BRON-to-sawr-us). This giant dinosaur was named "thunder reptile" because it made so much noise when it walked. It liked to eat pine needles, other plants, and was taller than many trees. It was 75 feet long, 15 feet tall at the hips and weighed sixty thousand pounds. Brontosaurus lived in the U.S.A. (Colorado, Oklahoma, Utah, Wyoming) and is also called Apatosaurus.

Diplodocus (dih-PLOD-oh-kus). This dinosaur had a very long neck and tail. It had a double backbone and nostrils on top of its head. It ate plants and may have lived in the swamp. It was 90 feet long, had a 26-foot-long neck and 45 foot-long-tail. It stood 13 feet tall at the hips and weighed fifty thousand pounds. Diplodocus lived in the U.S.A. (Colorado, Montana, Utah, and Wyoming).

Maiasaura (my-ah-SAWR-uh). This dinosaur had two legs and a duck bill. It was called "good mother lizard" because it was found near a nest of young. The babies were probably 14 inches long when they hatched and stayed in the nest until they were about 3 1/2 feet long. There were other nests in the area. This made up a dinosaur "nursery."

Othnielia (oth-NEEL-ee-a). This little dinosaur had a small head with large eyes. Its beak was lined with teeth. There were five fingers on each hand. It ate plants. It was the size of a turkey and walked on two feet. Othnielia lived in the U.S.A. (Utah, Wyoming, Colorado).

Pteranodon (ter-AN-o-don). This creature had a six-foot-long head, small body and a large 27-foot wingspan. It weighed about 33 pounds. It flew like a glider and ate fish. It may have been furry and warm blooded. Pteranodon fossils have been found in Kansas, U.S.A. (A fossil could be an old bone turned to stone; a stone bone!)

Stegosaurus (STEG-oh-sawr-us). This dinosaur was about the size of an elephant and ate plants. It had two rows of large plates down its neck. It carried its head low and its tail had four spikes. Stegosaurus was 11 feet tall at the hips, 25 feet long and weighed about five thousand pounds. It lived in the U.S.A. (Colorado, Utah, Wyoming).

Trachodon (TRAK-uh-don). This dinosaur had a wide duck bill and up to two thousand teeth. It ran on two legs and ate plants, fruits and seeds. It grew to be 14 feet tall, 30 feet long and weighed seven thousand pounds. It lived in North America and in England. Trachodon is also called Anatosaurus.

Triceratops (try-SER-uh-tops). This dinosaur had a short nose horn and two long head horns. It was called "Three-horned Face." It was 9 feet tall, 25 feet long and weighed ten thousand pounds. Triceratops roamed North America and had no enemies. With those horns who would want to be an enemy?

Tyrannosaurus Rex (tie-RAN-oh-sawr-us). The Tyrannosaurus Rex was king of the dinosaurs. The word Rex means king but there were lady Rexes too. He was 20 feet tall, 50 feet long and weighed as much as sixteen thousand pounds. If he lived today he could look into the second story window of a big house. His teeth were up to six inches long and he ate meat. His arms were too short to scratch his chin! Tyrannosaurus lived in the Western U.S.A. His fossils have been found in Montana, Wyoming, and Alberta, Canada.

Ultrasaurus (Ul-tra-sawr-us). This was the largest known dinosaur. It may have been 60 feet tall, 100 feet long and weighed 160 thousand pounds! This is fifteen times the size of an elephant. It was the largest known land creature that ever existed. Its legs were as big as a giraffe is tall. It ate plants (a lot of them!) and lived in the U.S.A. (Colorado).